Being Grateful, Being Thankful:
Appreciate Everything
For Even The Rain Brings Rainbows

by Sarah Butland

First Edition
ISBN 978-0-9937864-1-9
Published by:
ProSpec Industries Inc
PO Box 25100
Moncton, New Brunswick
E1C 9M9
Canada
http://www.ProSpecIndustries.com

ProSpec Industries Inc books are available at special discounts for bulk purchases for sales promotions, fundraising, or educational use.

Special editions or book excerpts can also be created to specification upon request.

For more information about the author, Sarah Butland, please visit:
http://www.SarahButland.com

Gratitudes

Introduction

Wherever you are in life, wherever you are right at this moment you have much to be thankful.

You likely hear the words "Thank you" as much as you say and hear the words "I'm sorry" in a day, but it's important to listen to it and say it with meaning. To truly be grateful is to appreciate where you are and where you've been, so that you can know where you will be going and as well as how to get there.

With the Law of Attraction being on everyone's mind, it seems the world still finds it challenging to think in the positive and be appreciative of where they are and what they have. If you struggle with this, or if you don't really, this book is for you.

Not every chapter may be relevant to you at the time you read it, I encourage you to read it. You may read the chapters in any order you choose; I do encourage you to read them all for greatest effect.

Why? Let's say, for instance, you don't currently have your drivers license, so at first you think it silly to be thankful for that. Take a moment and wonder if you would ever like to have your license. To have that independence and freedom to grab the keys and go when you're ready and not when you can afford a cab or at the whim of another driver. Reading this chapter now will send your intention to your future so it understands how wonderful you will feel when you have your license.

Life is about feeling- something science nor religion can ever truly explain. When you experience gratitude, even in just a small dose, your vibrations are on alert and you smile a little. Standing a little bit taller, you suddenly feel proud and good, no matter who you are, and in doing so reflect this genuine feeling back to others around you.

What would happen if everyone appreciated everything for their experience and what it had to teach them? Quite literally, the world is already filled with energy, so this would work to amplify that magnificence to eventually heal the world.

We all think we want more time in our day. Envy the younger generation for their ability to wake up playing and continue to play all day, if we'd let them. Many of us say we'd be able to play if only we didn't have to drain ourselves to pay the bills

This attitude stops now.

Unlike every other self-help book you read, enjoyed and promised to learn from that now sits on your shelf; Be Grateful, Be Thankful is a book that will have you smiling and passing on happiness and inspiration to those around you instantly.

With over 30 reasons to be thankful, you can use this as a daily meditation and practice one intention per day for an entire month or you can read it all in one day using it to increase your vibrational level to its maximum. I invite you to write a personal journal and/or a public blog about your new outlook on life before, after and during the reading of this book.

By reading this every day and putting the readings into practice you'll have hundreds of reasons to be thankful.

Recognize the value of this book by finally recognizing all you have to be thankful for.

At the end of each chapter I have included a mantra to give you an idea of how to say thanks simply and effectively. Say this or a like mantra out loud once a day or as often as you feel it.

As always, thank you for reading,

Sarah Butland

Thank You For Running Water

It is said that much of the universe's water produced is a by-product of star formation. A star's birth is known to be accompanied by a strong outward wind consisting of gas and dust. When this outflow of material impacts the surrounding gas, shock waves that are created compress and heat the gas which becomes water.

Water is a source of life for all of us. Being able to operate a tap to access this element so crucial to our lives is a wonderful aspect of what we do each day.

You may have a filter, prefer bottled or to get some cold water from your fridge but it's so close and within a short walk that you should rejoice with every sip. Being able to offer a drink to a passerby or to someone in your family with no other work than to go to a tap is magnificent.

It is said one can survive three days without water, though this would be with headaches, poor nutrition and low energy. You wake up each morning from just a few hours of sleep with a thirst for liquid and the purity of water is the best way to quench your thirst. H_2O is a molecule that contains one oxygen and two hydrogen atoms connected by covalent bonds and we are connected through water. Water is in everything; each skin cell, every plant you see, and it has no calories or nutrients but is filled with essential minerals for life.

Appearing in our world in all three states of matter (gas, liquid and solid), water tastes like nothing and smells like nothing and is referred to as the universal solvent.

Water is a miracle that we take advantage of everyday without much thought that we can control at our own will and replenish in our system as it needs.

We boil and steam vegetables in it, cook protein in it, bake with it, swim in it and shower in it. An average daily activity for almost everyone you know is to turn on the hot tap, step under the spray and enjoy the 10 or so minutes of pure shower bliss. Revitalizing our skin and starting our day, showers have become so automatic that most of us only realize we need or want one when the water is turned off.

Coffee, or another source of caffeine you like, seems to be for humans as what gasoline is for cars and all contain water.

That quick and easy lifeline we all seem to tap into wouldn't be so wonderful if we had to leave the house in jammies to get it.

What do you think will happen when the whole world thanks the universe for accessible and available clean water? Those who know, walk miles just to carry heavy buckets filled from a community well are so grateful each day that their bodies allow them to do that and there is water still in the well for them.

Camels walking through dry desserts for days at a time feeling grateful for the volume each of their humps have stored.

Laundry happens almost daily for you but it wouldn't be so easy to just push that button on your washer if there wasn't water hooked up to it. Imagine, just for a moment, taking your family's laundry basket to a communal water source hours away to spend the day getting your clothes a little bit cleaner. And now spend those hours appreciating what you already have that makes it a lot easier and more convenient to have clean clothes.

All of this happens for you. And we were able to dig a well, install the pipes, and run a tap to source this water so that you can wake up to have a shower or drink a glass of it.

A miracle you should offer thanks to from this day forward to notice how well it quenches your thirst.

Mantra:
Thank you running water for all you offer my life.

Thankful For Life

You are a miracle. How else would you describe the magnificence of starting from a tiny seed joining an egg, being accepted and cared for to be born months later. Complete with heartbeat, the ability to love and breathe, to see and be heard, your life begins with wonder.

In many religions, you are encouraged to wake up praising your lord for another day on the earth, to go to bed trusting the powers that be will do what is right by you to keep you safe and complete your life, however long that intends to be. No matter what religion or higher power you believe in, waking up each day is as miraculous as the life you were conceived to live.

You are born whole and continuously growing to have the ability to be complete in any form.

Life is something which gives you the ability to create the world you imagine. In a world with no limits, your birth was the beginning of a change only you can bring forth. Appreciating having your own individual opportunity to add value to a world so wondrous deserves personal praise.

You need to value yourself and know each of your days has unlimited possibilities. When you start each morning you have the opportunity to choose how your day goes by being thankful when you wake up instead of trying to hide under your blankets and delay your beginning.

You began when you were created, now it's your turn to develop and astound your parents with the same pride your parents felt when they first met you.

Your life right now may not be the most ideal or what you deem as perfect but this isn't because of you. With the pressure and expectations of society so many of us get lost. Being able to overcome that, to define our own path of success while being grateful for what we've overcome in our life and something to be thankful for.

Wake up each day grateful that you woke up, no matter how early it is or what you have planned. And, just for you, plan something amazing to look forward to. You were born years ago but now have the opportunity to be reborn based on your own expectations. You are in control now like never before so take at least 10 minutes, to sit outside in almost quiet, listening to the birds chirp or the wind whisper through the trees. Close your eyes and notice the smells, the sounds, and the music of all that surrounds you and breathe it in deeply.

Childhood songs rejoice in each element of what surrounds us, praising the green grass and the bird's nest on the branch as well as each snowflake that falls and through the years we somehow lose sight of that.

Our schedules and hectic lives sometimes gets in the way of understanding all that we have.

Each mosquito we hear feeds a bat which pollinates flowers and disperses fruit seeds, bringing food to other parts of the country and world. The healing powers of Aloe Vera, heat, shelter and shade from trees, the soothing power of the sea all contribute to our own humble existence which we have grown so accustomed to that we take for granted.

Nature exists in our lives in various ways that we can't even comprehend. Each cloud image we see reminding us of laying on our backs as kids, an acorn or root showing us that even the smallest of things can grow big a powerful. Rain contributes to each of these and gives us life both directly and indirectly.

This rain rids the earth of snow and ice and, especially after a long winter, this is welcomed and should be celebrated instead of dreaded.

If you have a garden, the time needed to water your plants is taken care of through April showers. Imagine for a moment having to walk to an ocean for water, to filter it and then disperse it to your flowers and family. Not many people would have the time or energy to go through that, especially without having your own water to drink.

The fish swimming in the ocean, oceans balanced with downpours, working to maintain nature's course each celebrate the water they swim in knowing they wouldn't survive without it.

It'll take practice to smile when the forecast calls for rain or when you get drenched in an unexpected downpour on your way to an interview. But just as much as you were brought up to cringe at the feeling of being rained on, you can teach yourself to rejoice in the sudden reminder of all that is wonderful.

Mantra:

I am grateful for each raindrop that falls to quench my thirst and maintain beauty in all that surrounds me.

Thanks For The Rain

Your plans for a picnic, soccer game or walk around the lake can continue even in the rain. The weather doesn't have to be dry, sunny and warm for you to enjoy what nature has to offer, you can enjoy it in all conditions.

Be grateful for the opportunity you have to go outside when you can and explore as much as time allows. While others are confined and look forward to their restricted access to a window, fresh air and the ability to walk on grass we take them for granted too often in our everyday life.

Don't wait for the moment when going to a beach or park is taken from you to appreciate the endless possibilities it allows. Go hug a tree now and feel both small and significant in what this world has to offer.

Take a few minutes each day, - you know you can find at least 10 - to sit on your deck in near silence, listening to the birds chirp or the waves splash against the shore. Close your eyes and notice the smells, the sounds, the music of all that surrounds you and breathe it in deeply.

Childhood songs rejoice in each element of what surrounds us, praising the green grass and the bird's nest on the branch, as well as each snowflake that falls. Through the years we somehow lose sight of that. Our schedules and need for money sometimes get in the way of understanding all that we have.

Each mosquito we hear feeds a bat which pollinates flowers and disperses fruit seeds, bringing food to other parts of the country and world. The healing powers of aloe vera, heat, shelter and shade from trees, and the soothing power of the sea all contribute to our own humble existence, which we have grown so accustomed to that we take for granted.

Nature exists in our lives in various ways that we can't even comprehend. Each cloud image we see reminding us of laying on our backs as kids, an acorn or root showing us that even the smallest of things can grow big a powerful. Rain contributes to each of these and gives us life both directly and indirectly.

This rain rids the earth of snow and ice and, especially after a long winter. This is welcomed and should be celebrated instead of dreaded.

If you have a garden, the time needed to water your plants is taken care of through April showers. Imagine for a moment having to walk to an ocean for water, to filter it and then disperse it to your flowers and family. Not many people would have the time or energy to go through that, especially without having your own water to drink.

The fish swimming in the ocean, oceans which are balanced with downpours, working to maintain nature's course, each celebrate the water they swim in knowing they wouldn't survive without it.

It'll take practice to smile when the forecast calls for rain or when you get drenched in an unexpected downpour on your way to an interview. But just as much as you were brought up to cringe at the feeling of being rained on, you can teach yourself to rejoice in the sudden reminder of all that is wonderful.

Mantra:
I am grateful for each raindrop that falls to quench my thirst and maintain beauty in all that surrounds me.

Yes, Even Be Thankful For Winter And Snow

So many of the people living around the Maritimes or in Canada in general, throughout the world in northern areas, complain about Mother Nature when the temperatures grow cold and the forecast calls for snow.

Winter tires, mittens, boots and slippery roads all come together to make people crankier than most days. Instead of being nervous and dreading going out in the cold, why not bundle up and enjoy the adventure.

One winter I kept promising my four year old son we'd go out to build a snow man. He declared building a snowman was his favourite part of winter and we had some making up to do from previous years. But circumstances and hesitation prevented us from getting out there until the very last minute. While others were complaining about the extended winter, we were out having the time of our lives taking advantage of the time and perfect conditions to meet our goal.

Snow and ice are not only there for us to appreciate the dry and warm weather but to fully enjoy. Outdoor skating, sledding, snow shoeing and sleigh rides are all parts of what should make you thankful for the coldest season of the year.

Then there's ice fishing, the warm nights by a fireplace while the snowflakes fall all around your house making a beautiful blanket of white on that very first snowfall. A Christmas, if you celebrate the season in any way, is ideal if it's a white one. While you listen to carols and see the snow gently cover the ground, appreciate the season for all that it has to offer you.

Mantra:

When it snows the earth glows and so do I. I am grateful for snow.

Be Thankful For The Sun

For most of you this is easy. With sun comes suntans, beach days, vacations, bonfires, and camping with friends and, of course, that much needed vitamin D.

Waking up to a sunny day is what most of us dream about. Getting out in a t-shirt and shorts and sporting the sunglasses to breathe in the scent of nature. Being able to open our windows to air out our houses, hang clothes on the line and eat supper on the deck is a dream come true.

In some places the sun is too hot and people pray for rain. The grass is brown, flowers are wilted and the earth is thirsty for hydration. Having the luxury of cool shelter and a refreshing glass of water is what some dream about. It's important to be thankful for the sun for all the reasons you can think of when it shines and is well balanced with rain and cool nights.

The sun brightens our days, gives the world colour through flowers and oxygen through trees. Its brilliance grows our natural food and warms our water, creating a wonderful world for us to live in. The tulips, evergreens and grass that always seem greener on the other side is all because of the sun.

So be thankful for all it does for you even if it is hiding behind the clouds today.

Mantra:

Thank you, Sun, for all the beauty you create in this world for me.

Flowers

Even dandelions have their place in our world and though most of us consider them to be weeds, they are in fact a beautiful flower meant to be rejoiced. The striking yellow against the green of grass is an abundant reminder to see beauty everywhere around us.

Remember that dandelions have the ability to spring back with more abundance than before like you can from a first rejection. Resilient in the toughest of days, it can be used for wine or kept on your lawn as a daily reminder of how you can overcome obstacles.

Arousing our senses with their scent and sight with their vibrant colours, wildflowers fill our paths with brilliance and influencing our mood. Gorgeous flowers with colours any bride can hold with pride, each having its own unique look and characteristics and all needing love, sunlight and water to grow.

Naturally growing or planted in a garden, flowers improve our moods whether we reflect their brilliance immediately when we see them or dry them to remember later. If we are gifted flowers we feel so good inside we don't focus on the colour or where to put them, we enjoy their beauty and relish the attention.

Not everyone can walk outside on a spring day to see flowers, even dandelions, on their lawn or walk in the park. If you can, be thankful for these moments of life's celebration. Enjoy the bees that pollinate the flowers and make honey from their essence and understand that you can make sweetness from on your own essence when you are joyous for many reasons.

Mantra:

Thank you, Earth, for filling my sights with the beauty of a variety of flowers, including the abundant dandelions, every day on every corner.

Technology

We often want to kick our computer or scream at when it's not working. And if we focus and dwell on it not computing as fast as we'd like, connecting as smoothly as we expect or following our commands as we need we'll have tools that work.

Instead, turn your focus on the days your power is on and your computer is working as it should. Learn a new computer course or ask a technology expert to explain an aspect of your computer you use every day you but don't fully understand. Realize how quickly you can access a wealth of information through a few keystrokes or call a friend by dialling 7 digits because of technology.

Technology is a path to advancement and as aspect of life that makes it easier to connect and stay in touch with otherwise lost friends. Development has made it easy to send a message to a loved one, wish them a happy birthday and invite them to an event. The Internet makes it simple for you to share the growth of your family to long distance family and friends with pictures.

Appreciate what you have while you have it instead of fearing your computer will not work as it's been low on memory or you've had problems with it in the past. Enjoy the version you have now even if it's a few years old as it is providing you everything you need and when it fails, that's a sign to take a step back and rejoice that it has been working for you. Or an Shift your focus and come back when you're more appreciative of what it has been doing and helping you accomplish.

Mantra:

I appreciate the technology I have for what it is and makes available for me.

Paying A Bill

Most of us cringe when it comes to some bills such as property tax, power, or an exorbitant phone bill, which only causes more aggravation and unnecessary payments. What we focus on becomes what our life is.

What you associate with an action speaks volumes for what will happen in your future. If paying a bill causes pain you'll feel like you're always paying bills and each is getting worse to pay. Make the conscious decision to enjoy helping your community improve their services and that you had heat this winter and are helping the phone company succeed.

Forwarding your money for services rendered can be an enjoyable moment of your day. How easily it is now to pass on money to support other companies and take advantage of the services they offer which is something we do on a regular basis. Dreading affects us negatively by ensuring we always have more or bigger ones to pay, enjoying the payment and what we get from it makes it more rewarding and fulfilling.

Though we may feel we don't have enough money sometimes to pay it forward, we somehow do what we can to pay our dues for services rendered. Having the ability and means to do that is something you have to embrace. Worrying about it makes it worse, getting it done and being able to move on from the payment will reduce stress and concern from your life and make room for happiness and clarity.

Mantra:

While I pay this bill I appreciate the services I have received and the comfort afforded me through these services knowing my money is paying salaries and helping futures.

Your Job

What you do for employment now is teaching you something you will continue to value in your future. Appreciate the opportunities you have to grow, learn and connect through by working your current job and understand you are exactly where you are meant to be at this moment.

Change your perspective on all of the hours you're working for a pay check instead of a career. Understand that you're gaining experience, patience and other skills while taking home a pay check that is helping you create the world you're comfortable living in.

If you're working full time you spend, on average, eight hours a day away from your family doing something to bring in money to pay your bills. Some of you are lucky enough to be doing what you love, maybe with fewer hours or more and smiling through most of it. Either way, it's truly important to focus on the positive and be grateful you are employed.

Think, for just a moment, of all the people who were recently laid off, fired or simply can't find a job of any kind. Consider the disabled neighbor who is frustrated sitting home collecting unemployment because he can't easily get out of the house. These people would love to have your job, no matter the pay or hours involved. They want to do something to bring in a pay check and feel they are valued.

With your job you have a position many would love to have. You're earning a paycheck, meeting co-workers, making connections and gaining experience you wouldn't otherwise have. These skills and experiences will shape your future, improving it with every obstacle and accomplishment you endure.

Enjoy what you do in the hours you're working and appreciate whatever pay you do take home so that you can tell the universe you honour the position you're in and have learned what you need to already to be able to progress.

Mantra:

Thank you, Universe, for this detour on my path to becoming who I need to be and for having a job that will allow me to appreciate my career path more. This job I currently have is a stepping stone teaching me even more about myself so I know exactly what I want for the rest of my life.

Your Past

We all have drama and memories in our past which we feel shape our future. We may resent it or enjoy and miss it; no matter what we think of our past we need to be grateful for it.

All of the situations in your past, good and bad have created your present. Each circumstance you've lived through has impacted your personality and value system.

Being thankful for whom we were, what our parents bestowed on us and how we dealt with it means we can leave the past behind us to rejoice in the present. Some say they don't have regrets, though it's ok to. This means you remember your past and have learned from it and your past really is the most important lesson you'll need to live through.

Your past certainly doesn't define you but it does create your present and establish your values. Use these to enjoy your present and plan for your future. Remember the time you met your best friend and your soul mate, the time you suffered the pain of getting your scars and hid for so long because people weren't looking for you.

It all comes together to create the person you are today and who you dream to be tomorrow. As awesome as you feel your future will become, show as much appreciation to your past for setting the stage for your presence.

Mantra:

Thank you, Past, for all you've done to create the person I am today.

Credit Cards / Loans

You've been approved for a credit card or loan and have used it for more than you expected to. You depended on it to get through tough times and sometimes struggle to pay back more than the minimum payment or interest.

Imagine your life without them for a minute. You'd have to get rid of your car, the shoes you absolutely must have and buy fewer groceries and so much more. With this approved credit you've paid bills and bought other items to be able to design your lifestyle to be as comfortable as it is.

Though you often worry about being able to pay everything back, these funds have gotten you through many emergency situations and established your own credit history. Whether you used the funds for a car to get you to and from work, for a business to help you do what you love, to be able to travel or just for extra purchases, this opportunity to borrow funds isn't available for everyone.

And so, be grateful with every payment you make to pay it off. Even if it's just the interest, feeling thankful for the opportunity to be trusted with the funds and pay it back will improve your mood and opportunities beautifully.

Mantra:

I am grateful for the opportunity to pay back the money I borrowed and establish trust between myself and my money.

Appreciate Your Full Piggy Bank

Loose change adds up. You can put it in your kids' piggy bank or save some for yours but any small change put aside means you're rich. Ok, maybe not a millionaire by any means, but you'll have much more than you may think.

People around the world can't afford a piggy bank at all and some in your own community stand or sit on street corners begging for a quarter or a nickel. Giving just a little change would make that person's day and many mean the difference of a hot meal or no meal at all. Appreciate how quickly and effectively each bit of change can add up.

Some cities have paid parking at every corner. Needing some change so you can go see your doctor or return a library book requires you to always have some in your cup holder or replenish from your piggy bank. In a lot of households, likely yours, this isn't given much thought as you always seem to have something left between the couch cushions or in that coin jar you keep. And somehow, no matter how often you dip into it, you put in more so there's always enough.

Be grateful. Appreciate that you can give just a little bit and still always have enough for yourself.

Mantra:

I am thankful there's enough change in my life to sustain my everyday activities and provide me the luxury to give back.

Friends

We all have them, the unfortunate part is that it can take us a while to discover our true ones. There are school friends who promise to stay in touch in the years after graduation and work friends who help make a shift easier to get through; but then there are good friends.

Good friends don't need to see you every day to know you're thinking of them. They send you a message every so often just to catch up or ask for advice they can't get from anyone else. Friends who are with you through the good times and worst times and see who you really are through it all.

The most important aspect of having a friend is simply being one. Being the person others come to when they need someone to get them out of a lonely place or just to laugh with about some things others may not find as silly.

Being alone can help you be better friends with yourself and grow into the person you truly know you are; but it's when you can come out after weeks of being grumpy to find someone standing at your door that means the world. A quick or long hug, a shoulder to cry on and a hand to wipe a tear you didn't realize was there makes a friend someone to be grateful for in every moment.

And you may not have a good friend now, or think you don't, but one is waiting and needing you just as much as you want them. Being able to know who you are and appreciate that the next stranger you meet will share with you something you never had before is pure wisdom.

Mantra:

I am thankful for past, present, and future friends, for what they have taught me about myself and what I will continue to learn.

Family

We all have family. Love them or hate them; our blood line goes somewhere and our love for our guardians may be even stronger.

Some of us have parents or siblings that abused us in horrific ways but we have conquered to discover our true family who support, protect and love us. Many believe that a perfect family consists of two loving parent's and two kids who get along for the most part. We've learned it goes beyond this realm in many different ways.

An orphan being adopted by strangers from across the world, a young child abused by someone close and a newborn not quite latching to his mother's tit all find themselves through their family. Good or terrible, we belong to something greater than ourselves and are meant to rejoice into the family we love the most.

Look around you, not at the blood that determines your faith, but the family you have chosen to share your life with. These are the people you can depend on and cry with when times get tough, as well as rejoice with when those times pass.

Family will be with you until the end, whether or not they are linked through blood.

Mantra:

I rejoice in the family who surrounded me on the first day and through all the days in between. Grateful am I to those who believe in me and ensure I have something to believe in. Thank you, family, for I am everything with you by my side.

Your Home

All too often people grumble about only having one bathroom, having to do too much maintenance or having a lawn to mow. Stop for a minute, imagine your day without that. Snap your fingers and have this same home disappear, where would you be?

Ok, so you wouldn't have a lawn to mow, a drive way to plow or a roof to repair but where would you be without it? You'd probably be searching for a bench to shelter from the rain, somewhere to put your car without paying a fee and needing a park for your child to play in.

Appreciating all you've been able to find and cherishing it won't make the maintenance of owning your home go away, nor will it reduce your payments, but it will change your perspective and help you enjoy it again.

Remember that exciting moment when you were approved for your first home. That excitement when you found your dream home and you were able to move your belongings into it to make it your own. How did you feel getting the door to open with your brand new key and seeing your own castle open before you?

That moment of pure joy can and should be easily felt every day. A roof above your head, a door to close and a bed to sleep in – not everyone is as lucky as you to have such things. It takes work but what it provides is worth much more than the occasional plumbing call or struggle to deal with the bugs while mowing the lawn.

Mantra:

This home is my castle and I will do what I can for it as it does so much for me. I feel joy with each moment I'm inside, comfortable and safe, and will protect it in return for it protecting me.

School

Grade school, higher learning, a 6-8 hour day listening to a teacher- these all contributes to your higher learning and growth. There are lessons to be learned within each class that a student can use to establish their own future. Not every student will get along with every teacher, but here begins our journey of learning to think and evaluate.

This beginning is not as available around the world. Girls, in some countries, are not allowed to read, and are expected to stay home and manage the house. Imagine walking endless miles to and from your school room, stumbling along the way and not being able to afford to keep going – physically, mentally or financially.

In First World countries, even while this tragedy happens, people complain about the early and long hours involved with attending school and this is the worst tragedy in itself.

Teachers are wonderful people dedicated to ensuring you experience many subjects in order to find your passion and feel fulfilled. As a student, even a disagreeing one, it should be easy for you to understand what has been made available for you, a journey for you to succeed and be tested in many ways.

School is available to many as a way to connect with people of all ages and begin to understand the world. It is a way to understand the value of everything in our lives through the opportunity to learn from many others, both teachers and students.

Mantra:

School for me is a place for me to feel safe, learn and establish who I am. I am thankful for the teachers, fellow students and the environment in which I'm challenged to question what I'm taught.

Pets

Animals of all kinds have an endearing and therapeutic quality to them – even the ones who make messes.

Indoor cats with litter box training still have accidents and get sick but, let's be honest, so do we. When messes occur it's important to remember all the joy they bring to your life. Consider a dog who comes at your call, greets you at the door and watches you leave – this dog may have chewed your favourite shoes but adores you like no other.

Shoes can be replaced and floors cleaned so always remember the initial excitement of adopting the pet you chose. Dwell on all the cute idiosyncrasies your pet has brought to your life.

Mantra:

This occasional mess pales in comparison to the joy this animal brings me. Thank you for all the good days (your pet's name) offers.

Customer Service

Our world requires us to depend on others many times
during each day such as calling to order something,
chatting to ask for advice or visiting a store or
restaurant for service. We approach complete strangers
and asking for something that makes our own lives
easier without giving much of a second thought to the
person who is helping us is something we are all
guilty of.

Memorable are the moments a retail salesperson
hovered or a waitress confuses our order but these
events shouldn't weigh upon us as much as we allow.
It is the moments of pure joy, eagerness to help and
honesty that is offered which we should remember.
These strangers are helping you so they can help their
family or pay a bill, with much more on their minds
then serving you and hundreds of others each day.

Yes, they are there to do their job, but we're all human
with many things on our mind at any one given
moment. A mistake is just a mistake. Don't blow it out
of proportion or complain to others of one silly
instance that can be forgiven. When you call someone,
buy something or ask anyone for help please thank
them. Appreciate all that someone else has to offer
you - a unique skill or profession that helps makes
your life easier.

As the saying goes, everyone is dealing with their own problems and it's up to you to ensure you're making the best of your own situation while trying to improve the day of others.

Mantra:

Everyone has the right to make a mistake and it is my right to let it slide, look past it and continue to make my own life great.

Obstacles

Failures, bumps in the road, hurdles, and rejection letters – no matter the form we experience, obstacles happen in all of our lives. We do our best to avoid them and are devastated when something keeps us from living our dream as quickly as we'd like, yet each brick wall is teaching us something.

The most common spin on this is that when one door closes another opens and it's true, it just might not be obvious. The door may be years down the road or a window with darkness on the other side which brings fear and dread into the mix. We all need to get out of the habit of focusing on what we asked for and focus instead, on accepting what life is offering, no matter the risk in this.

On the other side of a closed door is something far greater than you ever imagined. Today you didn't achieve all that you expected and it's for a purpose you may not understand at just this moment. Brush it off and realize all dreams do come true in the best way possible when you're willing to accept them for what they are.

"The brick walls are there for a reason. The brick walls are not there to keep us out. The brick walls are there to give us a chance to show how badly we want something. Because the brick walls are there to stop the people who don't want it badly enough. They're there to stop the other people."

–Randy Pausch, The Last Lecture

When you want something important to happen or change in your life, you will find a way to get through the door with all the experience you've learned from in your past. Want it and go for it.

Mantra:
This delay is teaching me something and I'll take a step back to find its lesson and improve my next step.

Time

We all have 24 hours in a day. It's what we do with each minute of each day that really matters. It's common to grumble out loud asking for more hours in a day. We get busy being a parent, a student, an employee, etc. and we just feel if we had another hour or day of the weekend our lives would be better.

This is a thinking error. Our lives can be great with the time that we have based on how we spend it. If you're wasting away watching your favourite weekly episode or complaining about your week, stop it. Take this time to shift your focus and make your life exactly what you want it to be. Appreciate that you do have 24 hours, 1440 minutes, 86400 seconds or 1 day to change your perspective and what you do with it.

Time is no one's enemy, wasting it is. Using a minute to its full potential by focusing, being aware, breathing and doing what you've put off for weeks will improve your life dramatically. Sitting and finding excuses, telling yourself the laundry can wait and then being annoyed with it in the morning is counterproductive. When you think of the laundry go put it away; it takes just a few minutes of your day, likely less time than you normally spend avoiding it, and makes you feel accomplished after.

Putting the laundry, dishes, sports gear, shoes away, doing whatever is haunting you, clears the clutter from your space for fresh thinking and greater success. It may not seem like much and there will always be some cleaning to do but when you get rid of the major clutter, new ideas start forming. Once you get one thing done since you're up anyway, you might as well go for that walk or change that light bulb.

Mantra:

I have 24 hours in my day and will spend them wisely ensuring I do things that propel me forward and improve my well-being.

Waiting

Though it may come as a surprise: **it's not all about the now**, not always. Being patient is crucial to letting your life unfold as it should and exactly when you're ready for it.

Life is similar to a good meal, it takes time to ensure everything is presented as perfectly as it should be. Get it too soon and you may not be prepared to enjoy it to its fullest extent. You may be working towards your dream and don't understand why you don't immediately see success, but it's coming if you keep working.

A tree starts as a small seed hidden underground and waits for the perfect combination of elements to present themselves. Rushing it will create havoc or kill it with too much sun or saturating it with water.

Doing something for it every day allows lets it to grow to its full potential. Each effort you put forth aligns your own compass to keep you on the right path.

Your journey is preparing you to appreciate the successes even more when they do arrive; so you know just how to receive each milestone and improve your chances of continued success.

Mantra:

The timing wasn't right for this success so I will wait,
try again and continue dreaming, striving and learning.

Ability To Drive

A right of passage for many, yet a scary and much delayed endeavour for others. Getting behind the wheel takes a lot of courage, more so when it's your very first time.

To be able to set your own schedule to get where you need to be is a freedom that comes at a cost – both financially and emotionally. Some of you were able to get your license as soon as you turned sixteen, while others waited, or are still waiting. Either way, if you're driving, now you understand the relief of not having to depend on others.

Be thankful you have the easy access to a vehicle, to be able to grab the keys when you need and go. Many people who are still too afraid or simply are not in a position to have a car. You should feel honoured you are trusted with such an accomplishment.

Mantra:

Thank you to the universe for the opportunity to learn and develop the ability to drive.

Your Vehicle

Oil changes, tire rotations, brake pads and gas are expenses and problems easy to complain about but none of these are really the end of the world. You will be able afford what is necessary for you to pay for and be able to replenish your bank account when you need it the most.

Your vehicle gives you the freedom you desire and protects you while you enjoy it. Keeping it maintained and in good service is crucial to ensuring it is there when you need it most.

A vehicle, like your home, should be appreciated for all the days it provides what you need. Grumbling about having to get maintenance done on it occasionally is silly in comparison to all the days you take it for granted. Start enjoying the days it gets you to where you need to go in time, take a moment to exclaim appreciation for its air conditioning or heat when you need it the most. Be constantly aware that every component of your vehicle works together at your command, starts and stops like it should and keeps you and your family safe.

The power of your positive thinking will ensure things continue to run smoothly for you and reduce the amount of time it needs in a garage, as such, saving you money.

Mantra:

I appreciate my vehicle for working as it should, as often as I need and at my command. The maintenance and safety inspection will go wonderfully as I have embraced the past month of having a safe vehicle to use as I needed.

The Success Of Others

A challenge for many is being able to celebrate and appreciate the achievements of others.

Another persons' good fortune doesn't come from their good luck or your own bad luck. Success, mine or someone else's, has more to do with persistence, dedication and focus. Being able to genuinely be happy for another person's reward and accomplishment humbles us and ensures we value the importance of all they've been through.

There's no such thing as an overnight success so before you judge, ask for their story. Singers, actors and writers have experienced rejection and triumphed by studying the greats so feel proud of those around you who have succeeded first.

Often times we think we are more deserving, proud of our own efforts and persistence but it's important to realize others are always striving for the same outcome. A candle doesn't shine any brighter than another but they are often lit at different times, at the very moment they are needed to light a path or another one is extinguished.

Being happy for someone else, honestly delighted for them, means you know they are deserving and you are close to someone you can learn from. Their modesty and support for others contributes to their own flexibility in life, to be able to adapt to the world around them and appreciate all that their journey has taught them.

Mantra:

I am genuinely happy for the success of my peers as it ensures I'm surrounded by greatness and wise people showing me the way to my own accomplishments. Their journey of struggles and triumphs has taught them how to be humble and how to appreciate others.

Ability To Read

With illiteracy rates ever a concern, having the ability to read a recipe, book, letter, even your bills is something to be grateful for. As we do it often a lot of us take this task for granted when there are people in your own community who can't drive, bake or grocery shop because they can't wrap their minds around enough words to make it possible.

You may not always have the time to read a novel but most parents do find the time to read a book to their child. A vital part of parenting, being able to read a book aloud and encourage the love of books in your children, which also works your own brain.

Dreading the mountains of paperwork you have to get through today at work? Take a moment and realize that not everyone you know is able to accomplish it.

Enjoy your talent that allows you to read each word, make sense of the whole sentence to be able to get your job done.

What's your favourite board game to play with your family and friends? Most require even a little bit of reading, even if it's just the directions; if it looked like it was in a foreign language you didn't know, you'd be frustrated before rolling the die.

Education is something we can all enjoy. That dreaded book assigned by your high school teacher, the exam you have to study for and the application you need to prepare for your dream job all need your ability to read to accomplish.

And with that appreciation for reading comes a big responsibility. One that not everyone can enjoy so to have that is a miracle in itself. Though you may not think you have the time, think for a moment how long most tasks would take you if you struggled to make sense of the written word. Understand how many people are embarrassed to say they can't read while they maintain a job, family life and get food to eat.

Then you'll appreciate how easy it is for you to quickly get through the paperwork, buy your lunch and read to your child. Then you'll know how rewarding taking just an hour a week to help a struggling reader discover their love for reading.

Mantra:

I am grateful for the ability to read every word presented to me in a day. With reading I was able to easily enjoy this book, find my dream job, apply for it and teach others the magnificence of the written word.

Ability To Write

Not everyone can put a sentence together or take paper to pen to form a coherent thoughts. You can, and in doing so, have the power to leave a legacy. Your words will be part of history, a story you can leave behind for generations to follow. Make the message count and worry less about the proper flow of things.

Many readers fail to leave a review, convinced they are not a writer and can't be as poetic or structured as the book to do it any justice. Opinions matter more than how they are said- it matters that you say them.

Being expressive with words, and encouraging that in others will leave a legacy even you can be proud of. Whether you're on Twitter coining a phrase in 140 characters or writing a novel, we're all told each of us has a story within us. Writing is a form of communication that can change our world. Even if no one reads what we have written, being able to pour our soul out in a journal kept private changes us and thus helps us better ourselves and the people we touch.

Writing is not all Shakespeare, Poe and Atwood but it's important to write or tell our story because we can. Many people who struggle with the ability to write at all look up to those who can write to share their story with the world. Rejoice in the idea that you can help others share their message.

Mantra:

Thank you for the education and passion I have to be able to write what I can to bare my soul and leave something behind.

Your Spouse

You fell in love and found many reasons to move in with or marry the person you did. No, you may not have known they leave socks on the floor or dishes on the table, but those are things you'll need to adjust to for the greater good of yourself and the relationship. Trust me, you have annoying habits, too that irritate your loved one.

Love is special and love is kind even though we may need subtle reminders on occasion. Focus on everything your spouse does for you, like sharing a blanket or playing with your children. In the grand scheme of things, a pair of socks on the floor really doesn't compare to the magical memories you've created with your last trip or the feeling you get when you hold hands.

Tell the world how wonderful you felt when breakfast was made for you, even if you needed to clean up afterwards. Share how you were welcomed home after a long day of work or how your spouse listened to you grumble about your seemingly dramatic day. You'll see, very soon, these cranky days will be fewer and farther between when you recognize all the good in them.

You'll still have bad days, get annoyed by the forgetfulness of your loved one and want to run away, but you can help that. The bad day you're having is the result of your focus on that forgotten thing, but if you simply take care of it yourself or give a gentle reminder, all will be well.

Your well-being directly affects those around you so leave work at the office and feel relief when you walk in the door and supper is made or a hug is to be had. Spread your news of the soft embrace and let that go viral so others start seeing more amazing stories throughout their day.

Mantra:

I fell in love with my husband for intellect, romance, and sense of humor. That is all still there as we grow closer and experience more. Thank you, Universe, for bringing him to me and keeping us together so I can love, feel loved and share love.

Conclusions / Endings

It can be difficult to near the end of something, to know an adventure is over and done with but it doesn't have to be. The end of one thing is just the beginning of something else.

In Being Grateful, Being Thankful, I shared with you many aspects of life that are often a struggle to appreciate but should be; conclusions being one of them. But like many aspects of life you graduate from, this book really isn't over, it has only just begun.

Now that you're just about done reading it, I want you to consider how you can change your own perspective in many aspects of your life. Don't wait to be tagged in a "Positive Chain" and feel obligated to post three positive events for three days to be able to tag another. Just post them.

Refrain from grumbling about the cost of gas, having to change plans due to rain or getting up too early. Rejoice in the way your life is unfolding before you and share your tips on how to save gas, your adventures in the rain and how you accomplished so much in your day based on that extra hour you found.

Once you get in the habit of telling your friends how awesome your life really is, it will become even better as your friends will start realizing how awesome their lives are.

So go do it now, don't delay. Live your life with a smile and a positive thoughts. A smile is contagious, we all know that, but energy and a vibrant life is, too.

Mantra:

Though this is the end of this, it is the beginning of something greater.

Appreciations

Being Grateful, Being Thankful in paperback would not
have been possible without the financial help from:

Tracy Nickerson

Jason Lawson

Carol Bird

Colleen McKie

John Tighe

Andrew Heighton

Jennifer Leadbeater

Dorothy A Lecours

Bonnie Rose

Tony Vrensen

Terrance Trites

&

Stephanie Marin

To each I owe much more than I can ever repay.

Thank you, to all of you, who travelling this journey with me and
shared, supported, commented and will buy my books in the future.

With many thanks to:

Kate Evans (www.beingandwriting.blogspot.com) for taking the right picture at the best time and sharing it with me. When imagining this book I saw a rainbow on the cover and she gave me two. Please visit her site today!

ProSpec for dealing with my high expectations & meeting them all.

Editors include Kelsey Jane, Cool Beans Editing
Reverend Terrance Trites &
Melissa Manes my new fabulous Beta Reader!
Heather L Tapia for all she does for empowering woman.

And, of course, my husband and son for the love they mirror.

If you enjoyed reading Being Grateful please consider reviewing it on Amazon and Goodreads.
It doesn't take long to write and will mean the world to me!

Also look for my other books including a collection of short stories in Brain Tales – Volume One, Blood Day The Short Story, Arm Farm and my children's book, Sending You Sammy which introduces a new superhero – BananaBoy!

Also check out my website at www.SarahButland.com for news about my works in progress and to say hi!